Fun Fitness & Learning

55 Large Group Activities and
47 Hands-On Practice Pages
to Energize and Teach Young Children

by
Sabena C. Maiden

illustrated by
Vanessa Countryman

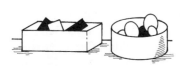

Publisher
Key Education Publishing Company, LLC
Minneapolis, MN 55438
www.keyeducationpublishing.com

CONGRATULATIONS ON YOUR PURCHASE OF A KEY EDUCATION PRODUCT!

The editors at Key Education are former teachers who bring experience, enthusiasm, and quality to each and every product. Thousands of teachers have looked to the staff at Key Education for new and innovative resources to make their work more enjoyable and rewarding. We are committed to developing educational materials that will assist teachers in building a strong and developmentally appropriate curriculum for young children.

PLAN FOR GREAT TEACHING EXPERIENCES WHEN YOU USE EDUCATIONAL MATERIALS FROM KEY EDUCATION PUBLISHING COMPANY, LLC

About the Author

Sabena Maiden is a former preschool and middle school teacher who taught for more than 10 years before making the move to publishing. She was hired by a leading educational publisher as a copywriter in advertising and later transferred to product development to work as a book editor. Since starting a family, she is now a freelance writer and editor. Having helped produce dozens of books, her work primarily includes educational, Christian, ESL, and literacy publications.

Dedication

To my husband and children who teach me every day how to love, live, learn—and keep me moving.

Credits

Author: Sabena C. Maiden
Publisher: Sherrill B. Flora
Illustrator: Vanessa Countryman
Illustrations on page 8: Chris Olsen
Editors: Debra Olson Pressnall and Karen Seberg
Cover Production: Annette Hollister-Papp
Page Layout: Debra Olson Pressnall
Cover Photographs: © Comstock, © ShutterStock, © Digital Vision, and © Photodisc

Key Education welcomes manuscripts and product ideas from teachers. For a copy of our submission guidelines, please visit our Web site or send a self-addressed, stamped envelope to:

Key Education Publishing Company, LLC
Acquisitions Department
7309 West 112th Street
Minneapolis, Minnesota 55438

Copyright Notice

Standard Book Number: 978-1-602680-81-4
Fun, Fitness & Learning
Copyright © 2010 by Key Education Publishing Company, LLC
Minneapolis, Minnesota 55438

Table of Contents

Introduction

As an early childhood educator, you know the best way to learn is by doing. Well, *Fun, Fitness & Learning* is all about "doing learning." This book is meant to help students become active while engaging their thinking processes. In preschool and kindergarten, most children are so excited—and so ready—to learn. How about harnessing that good energy and making it work to enliven your lessons! There are plenty of moments for students to sit at their tables and focus quietly on what you are teaching. And, that is important. However, many lessons that teach vital life and academic skills can also get kids moving while learning and thoroughly enjoying it.

Fun, Fitness & Learning is designed to build children's knowledge through action and high interest activities. Motor tasks and cognitive activities have been developed for the following topics:

- All About Me
- Learning the Alphabet
- Basic Concepts (Directional Words, Patterning, Go Togethers, Rhyming Words, Opposites)
- Identifying Colors
- Recognizing Emotions

- Using the Five Senses
- Moving Our Bodies to Be Fit
- Numbers & Counting
- Thinking About the Seasons
- Identifying Simple Shapes
- Community Workers

Each theme in this resource is comprised of five large-group movement experiences. Educators can use these activities to strengthen students' cognitive skills while fostering their motor planning, body awareness, visual memory, and gross motor skills. Most of the large group activities can be done in a classroom, but some of the games will require space to move or run around. If a large, safe indoor space is not available, complete those activities outside on a sunny day. Suggestions for locomotor movements are provided; it is best to vary the movements to keep children engaged in the activity. Locomotor movements include:

- gallop
- hop on one foot
- jump
- leap
- march
- skip

- slide feet to move sideways
- stomp
- tiptoe
- waddle
- walk

Accompanying most of the large group activities are reproducible half pages for individualized hands-on skill practice. Special attention has been given to fine motor, figure-ground discrimination, prereading, and math skills to prepare young learners for more challenging academic work.

Improving overall fitness and motor skill development while fostering readiness skills is possible. So, get your students moving; get them learning with activities from this book!

I Am Special Because I Can . . .

Begin by talking with the children about how special each one of them is. Discuss the fact that everyone brings a unique personality and individual talents to the class. Explain that you are all going to introduce yourselves by sharing one special physical talent. Give students some examples, such as jumping up really high, a forward roll, or a jumping jack. Then, share one of your own physical talents. Say, "I am special because I can . . ." and demonstrate your talent. Finally, invite students to take turns sharing their own unique physical talents.

Have students complete the worksheet below by drawing a picture of themselves. Then, post the artwork on a bulletin board titled "Look What We Can Do!"

Name

 Draw a picture about yourself.

I am special because I can . . .

Charade Parade

Start by explaining the basic rules of charades. Tell children they are going to play a game where each player will take a turn to act out his favorite indoor/outdoor activity or something the child does during the day. Emphasize that the player cannot say anything but must only use hand and body gestures while the class guesses the activity. Provide an example round by acting out something you enjoy doing. (Note: You may wish to copy the pictures below onto card stock and use them when a child cannot think of an activity to pantomime.) Alternatively, have the children depict only outdoor activities.

Pictures shown: Boy eating his lunch, child resting, girl washing hands, boy reading a book, girl painting a picture, boy writing his name, girl dancing, boy playing the xylophone, girl playing the maracas and boy playing a drum, child building a sand castle, boy blowing a bubble, child jumping rope, boy pretending to be a firefighter, girl swinging, girl hopping, child playing soccer

Head, Shoulders, Knees & Toes

Introduce the activity by talking to children about the fact that different parts of their bodies have different important functions. Ask students what special work their eyes do. How about their feet? Then, tell the children that they are going to get moving and grooving while pointing out those parts. Teach students the classic song "Head, Shoulders, Knees and Toes," sung to the tune of "London Bridge," and encourage them to use active motions when naming and touching each body part. As students become familiar with the song, speed up the tempo till they are moving and laughing as they learn.

Head, Shoulders, Knees, and Toes

Head, shoulders, knees, and toes,
Knees and toes,
Knees and toes,
Head, shoulders, knees, and toes,
It's my body.

Make up other verses to sing, for example:
Eyes, ears, mouth, and nose, . . .
Elbows, knees, hands, and feet, . . .

Name

To the Teacher: Have child cut pieces of yarn and glue them to the plate for hair and eyebrows.

Make a Face

Color and cut out the pictures. Glue them on a paper plate to make a silly face.

My Family

Discuss with students how they communicate with their families at home through talking—using spoken words. Tell them that they are going to learn another way to "talk" by using special hand gestures called American Sign Language (ASL). Demonstrate each of the following ASL signs as shown below. Allow students to practice the signs in class. Then, have students stand as you teach them the following song to the tune of "Mary Had a Little Lamb." Encourage them to use the family words that describe their own households. Finally, invite them to teach both the signs and song to their families.

I Love My Family

I love my family,
Family,
Family.
I love my family,
Mommy, Daddy, my [sister(s), brother(s), etc.]
and me.

I/me	love	family
Use right pointer finger to point to self.	Crisscross wrists and lay them on the chest.	Make the letter *F* with both hands and then rotate hands to touch small fingers.
dad	**mom**	**sister**
Use the thumb of the open hand to touch the forehead.	Use the thumb of the open hand to touch the chin.	Make the letter *A* and stroke the side of the cheek. Then, quickly bring pointer fingers together while pointing forward.
brother While holding the hand with palm down near the forehead, open and close the fingers a few times. Then, quickly bring pointer fingers together while pointing forward.	**grandpa** Use the thumb of the open hand to touch the forehead. Then, move the hand forward in small arcs.	**grandma** Use the thumb of the open hand to touch the chin. Then, move the hand forward in small arcs.

Some Fun with 1-2-3 Movements

Here is a great way to boost self-confidence—give each child an opportunity to suggest a favorite locomotor movement for this game. Divide the class into groups of three children. Choose one group to be the leaders. Start the game by having the first leader make a body movement (e.g., hopping on one foot) that represents himself. Everyone copies that movement. Ask the second leader to add a new movement (e.g., waving hands in air) that represents herself. The class, then, performs the first movement (hopping) on the count of 1 and the second movement (waving hands) on the count of 2. Finally, direct the third leader to show another movement (e.g., touching toes) that represents himself. Have the class perform the three movements in order while chanting the numbers 1, 2, 3. (If you prefer, say, "first, second, third" or "first, next, last.") Repeat the sequence of movements two or three times before choosing a new group of leaders.

Repeat the game until all children have suggested special ways to move their bodies. Alternatively, each time the class plays this game during the school year, have children perform a different number of movements in the correct order to strengthen short-term memory skills.

Name _____

To the Teacher: Direct the child to look at the arrows when drawing the shapes. For additional challenge, the child can draw a green triangle around the outside of each red triangle.

Use a red crayon to trace each large shape.
Use a blue crayon to trace each smaller dotted shape.

Fingerspelling & Musical Pillows

Arrange pillows in a circle (for the initial setup, you will need pillows for half the number of children in the class minus one). Select half of the class to form a circle around the pillows. Have the remaining students sit near you so that they will be able to watch your cues to start and stop singing. Explain to the players that you and the remaining children will sing the "Alphabet Song" (and fingerspell the alphabet) while they walk around the circle of pillows. When the music stops, they must quickly sit on the available pillows, one student per pillow. The student left standing will join the singers for the rest of the round. After each round, remove a pillow so that there is always one fewer pillows than the number of players. Continue the game until there is only one player sitting on a pillow. Have the first group of singers become the players for the second round while the other children sing and fingerspell the alphabet.

a	b	c	d	e	f	g
h	i	j	k	l	m	n
o	p	q	r	s	t	u
v	w	x	y	z		

Alive with the Alphabet

Children can learn the shapes of letters by making letters of the alphabet with their bodies, similar to yoga poses. Have children spread around the room. Demonstrate a chosen letter. For example, make the letter *T* by extending your arms straight out to the sides while standing tall and straight with feet together. For a challenge, have pairs of children work as a team showing alternate poses to illustrate each chosen letter.

Name

To the Teacher: Choose three letters and print them in the boxes to program the activity.

Trace, Print, and Make Letters

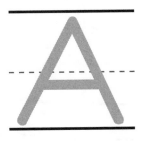 Trace the letter in the box with a crayon. Print the letter. Make it with clay.

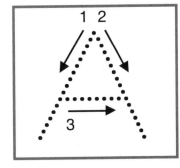

Letter Lineup

Beginning Activity: Prior to making the materials, decide which alphabet letters the children will practice identifying. (For example, match identical uppercase letters, identical lowercase letters, or an uppercase letter to its corresponding lowercase.) With a thick permanent marker, write and then underline each selected letter on a plastic foam ball and a large index card. Place a line of masking tape on the floor in an open area of the room. Arrange the letter cards along the taped line. Allow pairs of children to take turns picking up the prepared foam balls and hopping (or another locomotor movement) to the line to place the balls onto the matching letter cards.

Challenging Activity: Prepare game materials for practicing the entire alphabet. Print each uppercase letter on a plastic foam ball and each lowercase letter on a large index card. This time arrange the letter cards in alphabetical order along the taped line. Play the game in the same manner.

Note: To prevent the foam balls from rolling off the index cards, apply pieces of sticky-tack adhesive to the cards. Direct the children to place their lettered balls on the adhesive.

To the Teacher: On an enlarged copy of this page, write seven sequential letters individually with a marker on the train sections to program the activity. Be sure the selected letters are placed in random order on the small train cars. Make a photocopy for each child. Then, have children cut out and glue the parts in alphabetical order on another sheet of paper.

All Aboard the Letter Train

Cut out the pictures and paste them in order on a sheet of paper.

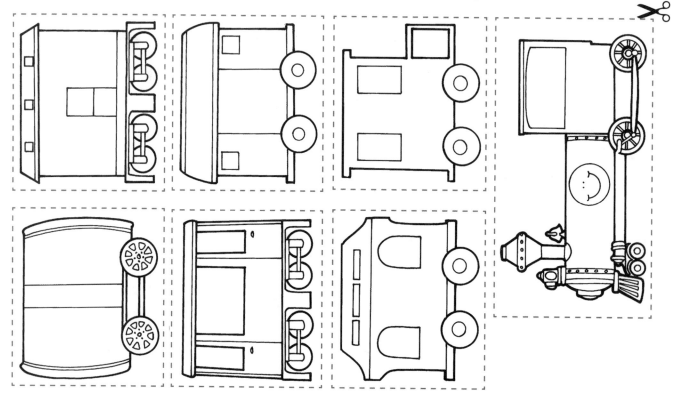

Letter Sounds

Teach children an action-packed version of the "Alphabet Song" using hand and body gestures. Have students sing and act out the lyrics to the tune of "Twinkle, Twinkle Little Star." Select a few letters from a set of alphabet flash cards. Divide the class into small groups and have each group represent a designated letter (skipping some letters each time). Sing the song, pausing for the group members to hold up their letter card, when its letter name is given, and say its phoneme. Next, the group members call out the name of an object or animal whose name begins with that letter (refer to the list if needed) and then pretend to be that object/animal.

Examples of Objects and Animals

A, /a/, apple	N, /n/, nail
B, /b/, basketball	O, /o/, otter
C, /k/, cat	P, /p/, pillow
D, /d/, dog	Q, /kw/, queen
E, /e/, elephant	R, /r/, rain
F, /f/, fish	S, /s/, snake
G, /g/, gorilla	T, /t/, tiger
H, /h/, horse	U, /u/, umbrella
I, /i/, insect	V, /v/, violin
J, /j/, jar	W, /w/, watch
K, /k/, kite	X, /ks/, X-ray
L, /l/, lobster	Y, /y/, yarn
M, /m/, moose	Z, /z/, zipper

To the Teacher: Make 26 copies of this page. Assign each child a letter to print in the box and then draw a picture of something on the clipboard whose name begins with that letter. Collate the pages into a class booklet. Alternatively, have children make their own letter booklets.

Name

Draw a picture for your letter.

My letter is . . .

Alphabet Animals

Encourage children to work on initial letter sounds while having some fun acting like animals. Introduce 10 or more animals (see below) to the class. Discuss the beginning letters of those names. Then, invite students to spread out in a large circle. Call up students one at a time and whisper to each the name of a chosen animal. Have the student go into the middle of the circle and act out the animal including any sounds the animal might make. If needed, announce the beginning letter sound/phoneme of the given animal's name to help children guess which animal is being depicted. When a child has identified the animal, she should state the beginning letter of its name. Play several rounds until every child has had a chance to be an animal. Alternatively, when the children are very familiar with the animals, have them guess the animal that is being depicted without any additional clues.

monkey

Examples of animals:
A—aardvark*, alligator, ant, ape
B—bumblebee, beetle, bird, buffalo*, butterfly
C—camel, cat, caterpillar
D—deer, dinosaur, dog, dolphin*, duck
E—eagle, earthworm, eel*, elephant
F—falcon*, ferret*, fish
G—gazelle*, giraffe, goat, goose, gorilla
H—hamster, hippopotamus, horse, hummingbird, hyena*
I—iguana*, impala*, inchworm
J—jackrabbit, jaguar, jay, jellyfish
K—kangaroo, killer whale*, koala
L—leopard, lion, lizard
M—manatee*, mole, monkey, moose, mouse, mule
N—newt*, night crawler
O—octopus, okapi*, ostrich*, otter, ox
P—panda, parrot, peacock*, penguin, pig, porcupine*
Q—quail*, quokka (short-tailed wallaby)*
R—rabbit, raccoon, rhinoceros, rooster
S—salamander, sandpiper*, sea horse*, seal
T—tiger, toucan*, turkey, turtle
U—umbrella bird*, urchin*
V—vole*, vulture*
W—walrus, whale, wolf, woodchuck*
X—X-ray fish*
Y—yak*, yellow jacket*
Z—zebra

toucan

okapi

*For lesser-known animals, discuss their names and provide a brief description of each before completing the activity. If possible, post the names and pictures of animals for children to review.

Game Variation: On the next page are pictures of some of the animals listed above. If interested, prepare picture cards as directed and place them in a small box. Have children act out animals shown on the cards. Whenever different animals are introduced to the class, add those pictures to this collection for children to use.

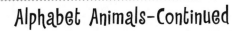
To the Teacher: Copy the pictures on card stock. Cut along the dashed lines. Write the corresponding alphabet letter on the back of each card.

Pictures shown: Row 1—ant, bumblebee, camel, duck; Row 2—elephant, fish, goat, horse; Row 3—jay, kangaroo, lion, moose; Row 4—newt, octopus, pig, rabbit; Row 5—seal, turtle, wolf, zebra

Over-Under-Over-Under

Divide the class into two teams and have each team stand in a line with children one behind the other. Give a playground ball to the first child in each line. When you say "Go," the first child passes the ball over her head and says, "Over." The next child passes the ball through his legs and says, "Under." Have each line continue the alternating ball pass until the ball gets to the end of the line. If the ball is dropped at any time, the team must return the ball to the front of the line and begin again. When the last child in line is holding the ball, she runs to the front of the line and announces, "Over, under, this game's over!"

Play variations of the game to teach other directional words such as top/bottom, up/down, above/below, and high/low.

Name _____

To the Teacher: For additional practice, have the child trace each path with a finger while saying the words *over* and *under*.

Follow the Path

Trace each path with a crayon. Trace again with a different color.

Moving for Patterns

For this patterning activity, gather blocks that are identical in size but different colors and place them in a large pile. Arrange a line of a few blocks in a simple recognizable pattern such as a red block, green block, red block, green block. Point out the arrangement of blocks that you started and ask children to identify which block color will be used next to continue the pattern. Repeat with a few more patterns, increasing the difficulty if appropriate. Then, have children sit on the floor side by side the same distance from the pile of blocks. Set up a new line of blocks in a recognizable pattern. Choose a locomotor movement and have children take turns performing the movement to retrieve a block from the pile to continue the pattern. Play several rounds as time and interest allow.

To the Teacher: Encourage the child to draw two or more shapes in each row.

Name

Think and Draw

Look at the shapes. Draw what comes next.

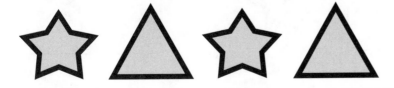

Matching Go-Together Cards

Pair off the children. Have them sit next to their partners on one side of the room. Choose five sets of matching go-together picture cards and scatter the cards individually faceup around the play area. (See the list of examples to make your own pairs of go-together photographic cards. You may also use a commercial set, such as Key Educationn's KE-845018 Things That Go Together.) Invite a pair of students to begin. Give that team a neck scarf with a large knot in each end. Have each child hold onto a knot as they work together to move (walk, skip, slide, etc.) around the area to find one set of go-together cards. Continue the game in the same manner until the five sets of cards have been collected.

Examples of Things That Go Together

baseball and bat	needle and thread
bread and butter	paint and paintbrush
burger and fries	peanut butter and jelly
cake and ice cream	pencil and paper
comb and brush	pillow and blanket
hammer and nails	pots and lids (covers)
hat and coat	shoes and socks
cheese and crackers	shovel and pail
iron and ironing board	soap and water
knife and fork	spider and web
lock and key	table and chairs
milk and cookies	toothbrush and toothpaste
moon and stars	

Name

To the Teacher: Let the child say the names of the pictures to a friend before doing the activity.

Match things that go together. Cut out and glue the pictures.

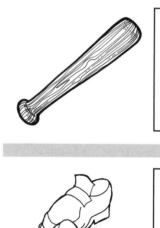   

Side-by-Side Rhymes

Pair off the children. Have them sit next to their partners on one side of the room. For this game, choose five sets of matching rhyming picture cards and scatter the cards faceup around the play area. (See the list of examples to make your own pairs of rhyming photographic cards. You may also use a commercial set, such as Key Education's KE-845014 Rhyming Pairs.) Have the children collect the cards in the same manner as the Matching Go-Together Cards game. Alternatively, have pairs of children gather actual articles of clothing, tools, toys, and other household items whose names rhyme.

Examples of Word Families

-ab—cab, crab	*-ick*—brick, chick
-ack—black, backpack	*-in*—chin, skin
-ag—bag, flag	*-ine*—line, nine
-ain—rain, train	*-ing*—king, ring
-ake—cake, lake	*-ink*—sink, pink
-am—jam, clam	*-ip*—lip, ship
-an—man, pan	*-ob*—cob, knob
-ank—bank, tank	*-ock*—lock, rock
-ap—cap, map	*-op*—cop, mop
-ar—car, star	*-ot*—dot, knot
-at—cat, hat	*-ouse*—house, mouse
-een—green, queen	*-ow*—cow, plow
-ell—bell, shell	*-ub*—sub, tub
-est—nest, vest	*-uck*—duck, truck
-ib—bib, crib	*-ug*—bug, jug
-ice—dice, mice	*-up*—cup, pup

Name

To the Teacher: Have the child say the names of the pictures to a friend before doing the activity.

Match things whose names rhyme. Cut out and glue the pictures.

   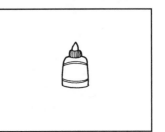

Simon Says with a Twist

Introduce the class to the concept of opposites with picture cards or actual objects. (You may prepare your own photographic cards by mounting pictures on index cards or use a commercial set, such as Key Education's KE-845007 Opposites.)

Play a round of the classic game Simon Says with students. Explain the rules before playing if needed. Tell the class that you are going to be "Simon." Explain that Simon will say and do an action, such as "Simon says, 'jump'." Remind children that they should follow Simon's direction only if the sentence begins with the words "Simon says." If the direction does not start with "Simon says," they should not complete the movement. Make the game as action-packed as possible to engage the class.

After students have demonstrated that they understand the game, tell them that for the next game you want them to do the opposite of Simon's instructions. For example, if Simon says, "Walk in place very slowly," the children should run in place really fast. Try to incorporate as many opposites as you can into the game—be creative, get children moving, and have fun! Examples of pairs of opposites include the following:

big/little	hot/cold	soft/hard
fast/slow	in/out	strong/weak
happy/sad	long/short	tall/short
heavy/light	many/few	thick/thin
high/low	smooth/rough	tight/loose

Name

To the Teacher: Have the child explain to a friend why the pairs of pictures are opposites.

Match things that are opposites.
Cut out and glue the pictures.

Call Out Colors

Version A: Have the class stand in a circle formation. Call out a color. If children are wearing that color, they remain standing. If not, they sit down. Toss a large ball around the circle to each child who is standing. Then, have the entire class stand up again. Call out a different color and repeat the game in the same manner. Continue in this manner until all basic colors have been named.

Version B: Create groups of approximately six children and have them form circles. Designate one child in each group as Player A. Give Player A a large ball to start the game. Player A names a color another child is wearing and then tosses the ball to that chosen child (Player B). Player B then names another color, tosses the ball, and so on. Continue playing until all colors of garments in the group have been named at least once. Then, form new groups and play again.

To the Teacher: Let the child also touch and count each balloon before working with paint to strengthen one-to-one correspondence skills.

Name

Think and Paint

With the tip of your finger, touch finger paint and then touch the balloons to fill them in with paint. Use more than one color of paint. Tell a friend the colors you used.

Color Quest

Ready to search the room for colors? To play this color game, provide colorful soft items, such as scarves, beanbags, or pillows. Place at least three objects of each color around the room. Keep things fun and safe by allowing just a few children to play each round. Have the players stand side by side. Then, give a direction such as, "Find one thing that is red" and the locomotor movement (walk, skip, gallop, stomp, slide, etc.) the players should use while searching for the item. When an object has been found, that player returns to the starting line. Play several times until everyone has had a chance to search for colors.

Name

To the Teacher: If the child cannot read the color words, use the crayon to draw the color cue under each word.

Think and Color

Use crayons to color the beach balls. Look at the key. Count the balls with a friend.

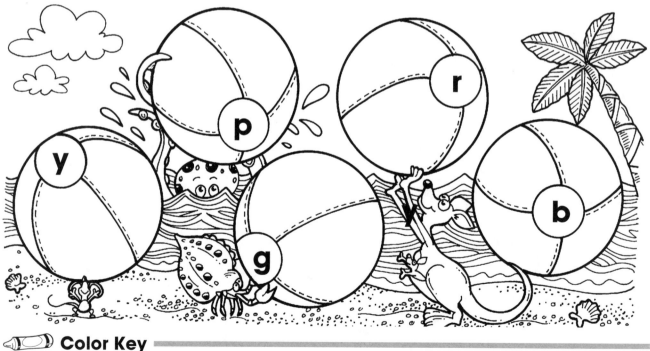

✏️ **Color Key**

b blue   **g** green   **r** red   **p** purple   **y** yellow

Balloon Bop

Reinforce the names of colors and strengthen eye-hand coordination with several games of Balloon Bop. Instruct children to sit on the floor close together in a circle. Tell them they will work together to keep one or two balloons in the air by gently patting a balloon upwards when it comes to them. As children try to keep a balloon afloat, have them sing the verse shown below about its color to the tune of "Row, Row, Row Your Boat." Play several rounds of Balloon Bop, each time using a different color of balloon to match the color words in the song's verse.

Note: Before completing any balloon activity, ask families about latex allergies. Also, remember that uninflated or popped balloons may present a choking hazard.

To the Teacher: Make a copy of the song lyrics below. Teach the class the song and then take the children on a nature walk. Each time a basic color is spotted, have the class sing the corresponding verse. Continue walking and singing until all verses have been sung.

Colors, Colors, Colors in the World

Green, green, green, green, green,
Gators, grass, and go,
What a nice color you are,
How I like you so.

Red, red, red, red, red,
Apple, bricks, and stop,
What a nice color you are,
You're always on the top.

Blue, blue, blue, blue, blue,
Ocean, sky, and jeans,
What a nice color you are,
You're fit for kings and queens.

Yellow, yellow, yellow, yellow, yellow,
Corn, cheese, and the sun,
What a nice color you are,
You're always so much fun.

Purple, purple, purple, purple, purple,
Eggplant, grapes, and plums,
What a nice color you are,
To you, I raise my thumbs.

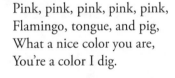

Pink, pink, pink, pink, pink,
Flamingo, tongue, and pig,
What a nice color you are,
You're a color I dig.

Black, black, black, black, black,
Tires, roads, and bat,
What a nice color you are,
To you, I tip my hat.

Brown, brown, brown, brown, brown,
Acorns, beavers, and dirt,
What a nice color you are,
Sometimes the shade of my shirt.

Orange, orange, orange, orange, orange,
Carrots, pumpkins, and juice,
What a nice color you are,
You have many a use.

White, white, white, white, white,
Snow, milk, and a tooth,
What a nice color you are,
You know it is the truth.

Colorful Moods

Begin the activity by talking with the class about the different associations and moods that a few colors seem to evoke, like yellow (sunny, happy) and blue (rainy, sad). Provide each child with six different colors of paper rectangles or pieces of fabric (red, blue, green, yellow, pink, and brown). Then, play different selections of music. After playing a short excerpt of each song, ask children to hold up the color that the song they are listening to makes them think of. Invite them to dance around according to the feelings they associate with the color. After each color dance, let children describe how they were feeling.

Alternatively, tape the ends of crepe paper strips to drinking straws or use commercial ribbon sticks and let children wave them while dancing.

- -

Name _____

To the Teacher: If the child cannot read the color words, use the crayon to draw the color clue under each word.

Stay on the Path

Use the matching crayon to trace the path. Color the picture.

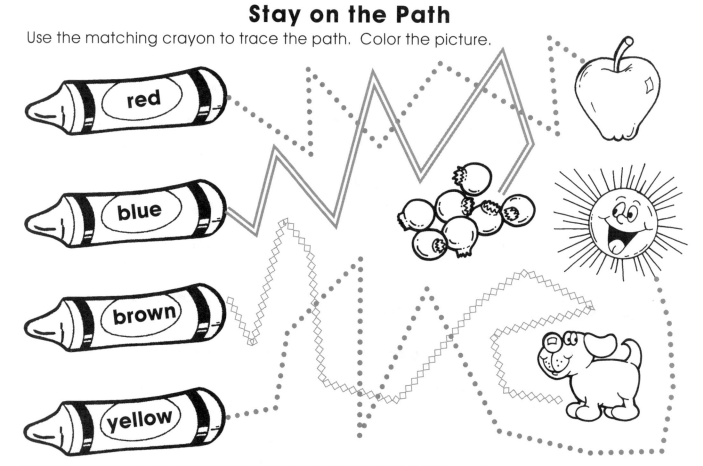

red

blue

brown

yellow

Red Light, Green Light, Go!

Start by playing a round of the classic game Red Light, Green Light with children. Explain the rules before playing if needed. One person will be the "stoplight" while the rest of the players compete to reach him. Have the remaining players form a side-by-side line about 15 feet (4.5 meters) away from the stoplight. The stoplight turns away from the classmates and says "Green light." When the stoplight is not facing the players, they may move towards him. At any time, the stoplight can say, "Red light!" and turn around quickly. If the stoplight sees any of the players moving after he has turned around, they must sit out the rest of the round. Keep playing until the stoplight has caught everyone or until one player reaches the stoplight; that child becomes the stoplight for the next round.

Alternatively, add more color to the game. Cut strips of construction paper in three different colors (excluding red) to create wristbands for children to wear. When the stoplight calls out a color, the children wearing that color may move forward by using a specified movement, such as "Blue light, hop!" "Brown light, crab walk!" or "Yellow light, tiptoe!"

Name _____

To the Teacher: If the child cannot read the color words, use the crayon to draw the color clue under each word.

Colorful Lights

Use the matching color crayon to trace the color word. Color the light.

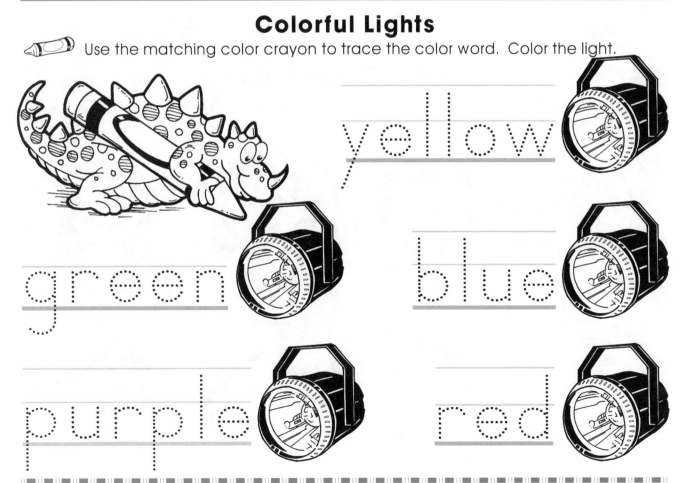

If You're Happy . . .

Teach children a version of the song "If You're Happy and You Know It," highlighting a variety of emotions. As children sing each verse, encourage them to act out the parts by exaggerating the motions as they dance around.

If You're Happy and You Know It

If you're happy and you know it,
Clap your hands.
If you're happy and you know it,
Clap your hands.
If you're happy and you know it,
Then, your face will surely show it.
If you're happy and you know it,
Clap your hands.
(Clap, smile, and skip or dance.)

Additional Verses

If you're angry . . . Stomp your feet.
(Stomp hard on the ground; make an angry face.)

If you're sad . . . Cry, "Boohoo!"
(Shake all over and wipe eyes as if crying.)

If you're frightened . . . Yell, "Oh my!"
(Look really scared, opening eyes wide, putting hands to mouth, and jumping back.)

If you're excited . . . Jump up and down.
(Smile and jump up and down.)

Alternatively, share pictures of people showing a variety of emotions before singing the song. You may prepare your own photographic cards by mounting pictures on index cards or use a commercial set, such as Key Education's KE-845001 Emotions.

Name

To the Teacher: Let the child point to the faces and tell you if they that look happy, sad, excited, or scared.

Look at These Faces

 Look carefully at the faces. Which faces show the same feelings? Draw a line to make each match.

Breathing for Better Feelings

Teach your students to use basic stretches and breathing exercises as helpful tools to understand and focus on their feelings. Try the following exercises with children and discuss how each exercise makes them feel. Talk about how focused breathing exercises can help them shift from feeling angry, anxious, tired, or frustrated to feeling relaxed, peaceful, energetic, or happy.

In and Out Breathing: Have children sit in a circle formation with small spaces between them. Tell the class to be very quiet and become aware of their breathing. Tell them not to change the way they are breathing, but to simply pay attention to how they feel as the air slowly goes in and out. Point out that while they focus on their breathing, they are relaxing their bodies. This kind of breathing exercise can help people to feel calm.

Tummy Puffs: Let children lie down on the floor on their backs with a small space between them. Direct children to place their hands on their tummies, take slow, deep breaths, and then exhale slowly or with several puffs. Ask them to pay attention to how their tummies move up and down. Explain that this kind of breathing exercise can help people feel better when something is bothering them.

Balloon Breathing: First, have everyone practice In and Out Breathing (at left). After a few moments, encourage the children to use their imaginations as they do the following steps:

1. Close your eyes.

2. Pretend you are a balloon.

3. Imagine that your breath is the air that helps you go up and down.

4. Breathe in through your nose so that you can lift up off the ground. (*pause*)

5. Let out the air by breathing out. (*pause*)

6. Imagine slowly coming back down to the ground.

7. Breathe in through your nose a little bit longer so that you can lift up even higher off the ground. (*pause*)

8. Let out the air by breathing out. (*pause*)

9. Breathe in through your nose a little bit more so that you can lift up to the clouds. (*pause*)

10. Let out the air by breathing out and feel all of the air gently go out from the top of your head to your toes. (*pause*)

After completing the steps, talk to students about how they feel. Do they feel peaceful and relaxed or energized and refocused?

Shake, Squirm, Giggle

Select a variety of music genres to play for children, choosing songs that might inspire many feelings. Begin the activity by talking about how music can "get the wiggles out" and that sometimes it can change a person's mood. Point out that music can even have the power to help people get over bad feelings, such as anger, disappointment, and sadness. After playing each musical selection, invite children to explain how the song made them feel. (For example, classical music can be calming or invigorating, country music can be energizing, techno music might inspire creativity, and so on.) Let children shake, dance, and express themselves while expending their energy and having tons of fun with the music.

Name

 How do you feel about each thing? Draw that face.

Feelings Freeze Tag

The classic game Freeze Tag is always a fun activity. Try this version with a twist. Before playing, explain the rules to the class if needed. Choose one person to be "it." "It" runs after the other students trying to tag them. When a child has been tagged, she must freeze, show a very sad face, and stay in the same position in which she was tagged. Once five players have been tagged, the round is over. The fifth person to be tagged will be "it" for the next round.

Alternatively, tell the class that whoever is "it" will choose an emotion and action, such as happy surfing, and call it out. As children run around to avoid being tagged, they must also make the chosen facial expression. If tagged, those players must freeze by holding their bodies to show the designated action as well as the specified emotion. The game continues as before. Explain that "it" can announce a different emotion and action at the beginning of each round. Brainstorm possible choices with the children before starting the game. Examples may include scared bicycling, curious skiing, and surprised skateboarding.

Note: For a follow-up class discussion, copy the patterns below on card stock, making one set for each child. Cut out the faces along the heavy line and mount them onto craft sticks. Each time the class plays this game, have children choose a face to show how they felt about participating.

Smelly Science

Set up three different stations in your classroom; in each station place a plastic, covered container holding a very distinct smell, such as cinnamon, vanilla extract, ground coffee, popped popcorn, onion, lemon juice, sliced orange, or peanut butter. *Note: Be aware of any food allergies or sensitivities your students may have.* Poke a few small holes in each container's lid. Place a different item in each container. Use a cotton ball if the scented item is a liquid. Explain that children will take turns to complete the smelling course by moving to the three stations in a certain way (skipping, sliding, tiptoeing, or hopping). After being at a station, the child will come back and whisper to you what was smelled in the container.

If the child incorrectly identifies a smell, she must take giant sized steps back to that station. After all children have gone through the course, talk about how they use their noses to smell various things.

Alternatively, set up a smelling center for children to investigate with a partner. Let them tell each other if they think each item smells good or bad.

Name

To the Teacher: Gather popcorn, a piece of ripe pineapple, and a slice of onion. Set up three special smelling stations. Have the child smell the numbered container holding the hidden item and then circle the corresponding picture.

The Nose Knows

What did you smell? Circle the picture. Then, draw any food that smells good. Draw any food that does not smell good.

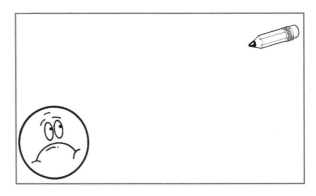

Taste Test

Gather two each of the following fresh foods: potato, white turnip, and apple. Prepare small cubes of raw peeled potato, peeled white turnip, and peeled apple. Cut each food the same size and shape so that they look similar. *Note: Follow school guidelines on serving foods in the classroom and be aware of any allergies or sensitivities your students may have.* Have children sit around a large table. Provide each child with a cube of potato; then, allow students to guess from the three choices which food they tasted. If they think they ate turnip, instruct them to hop to the front left corner of the room where you have placed an actual turnip. If they think they ate potato, they must crawl to another corner of the room where they can see a whole potato. If they think they ate apple, they must

sidestep to the back corner of the room where an apple can be touched. Continue the tasting activity with cubes of turnip and apple, having students guess the kind of food after each sample is tasted. Wrap up the discussion by talking about how their tongues allow them to taste sweet, sour, salty, and bitter foods.

Name

To the Teacher: Let the child tell a friend about the pictures drawn on the paper.

Tasty and Terrible Treats

Draw two foods that taste good. Draw two foods that do not taste good.

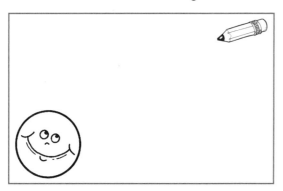

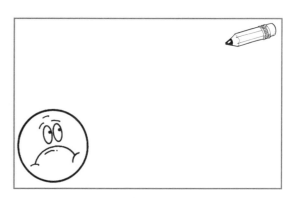

Bags of Fun

Fill several small plastic grocery bags, each with a different textured substance, such as dried beans, uncooked rice, cotton balls, or sand. Tie each bag securely with the handles. Then, double bag each one to ensure the contents do not spill. Have the students form two groups and ask them to line up side by side facing each other. Give one student a filled bag and let her toss it to the student standing across from her. That student then tosses the bag back to the second student in the first line. Have students continue to toss the bag back and forth until everyone has had a chance to catch it and feel the contents. Ask students to guess what is inside the bag. Repeat with each filled bag. End by talking about how they were able to use their hands to feel and guess each bag's contents.

Name

To the Teacher: Challenge the child by talking about how the feather feels smooth, the brick feels rough, and the mud can feel cool.

Touchable Things

Draw something that is soft, something that is hard, and something that is squishy.

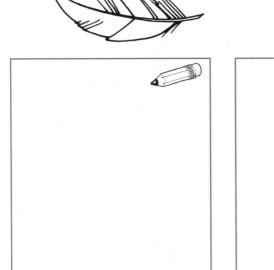

Tiptoe Tunes

Get everyone ready for this listen-and-move activity by having children line up side by side at one end of the room. Place a CD player on the other side of the room. Then, at a very low volume, play a familiar song. Have students tiptoe three small steps toward the CD player and then pause the recording. Ask if any of them recognize the tune. Resume playing the song and let children approach the CD player by taking three steps again. Continue the game in the same manner until someone guesses the name of the song correctly. Repeat the game using class favorites and other recognizable songs.

Name _____

Hear It!

 Draw a red circle around things that make a loud sound.

 Draw a blue circle around things that make a soft sound.

Before Your Eyes

Place four to six small common objects (one for each child in the small group), such as a toy, watch, comb, fork, etc., on a table and cover them with a tablecloth. Have children sit around the table. Announce that you are going to remove the cloth for 30–45 seconds while they look carefully at the objects. Replace the tablecloth and encourage each child to name an object that she remembers seeing on the table. After each student has had a turn to name an object, remove the tablecloth for 10 seconds while students look carefully at the objects again to see if the objects were correctly named. Then, replace the tablecloth and invite students to get out of their seats and dance around the table. Play some fun music and

lead them in a conga style dance for about a minute. Have students sit down and ask them to try to name the objects again. Play the game again with different objects as time and interest allow.

Name

Now You See It!

Circle the hidden things.

Picture Key

Fun with Fitness

Set up a fun indoor obstacle course with at least five physical challenges to complete. You could have children crawl under a table, stop and spin around three times on a mat, straddle jump over a pillow, do a log roll on very large carpet squares, and finish by hopping with feet together over a row of stuffed animals. Add a mixture of silly and challenging elements to make the course full of fun and fitness. Have students line up in single file so that they can take their turns individually; however, be sure to keep the action going. After the activity, let children talk about how much fun they had and remind them that while they were playing, they were also exercising their bodies. Talk about other fun ways to get exercise and how important it is to be active each day.

Name

Draw yourself doing your favorite exercise.

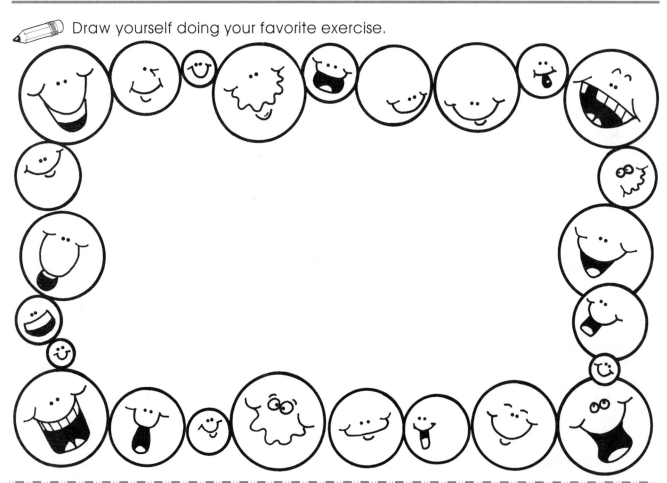

Healthful Foods

Place a large basket of food items (actual foods like fresh fruits, fresh vegetables, canned goods, and boxed convenience foods; empty cartons/sacks of frozen foods and snack items; food picture cards; or plastic food toys) at one end of the room. Label two bins/boxes: one with a smiling face for healthy choices and the other with a sad face for unhealthy choices. Place those boxes in the opposite end of the room. Divide the class into two teams. Have each team line up single file for a relay race. Explain that the first child from each team will power walk or skip to the basket of food, choose a food item, carry it back to the boxes, and then place it in either the healthy choices box or the unhealthy choices box.

After students have dropped food items in the boxes, they will give the next students in line high fives and then walk to the back of their lines. Only when the next students in line are given that signal can they take off to continue the relay. After everyone has participated, review as a class the contents of each bin. Discuss any misidentified foods, such as a candy bar being placed in the healthy choices box.

Name _____

Making Good Choices

 Draw a green circle around healthful snacks to eat.

Draw a red circle around snacks that are not healthful to eat.

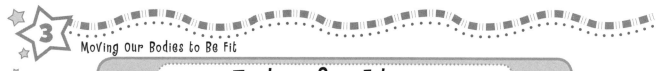
Testing for Fitness

Discuss with children that they are growing bigger and stronger every day. Talk about how the decisions they make daily for eating good foods, sleeping enough hours, and exercising their bodies can help them grow even better. Explain to children that they are going to do a fun fitness test. Demonstrate each exercise and then let each child complete it. Mark the children's efforts on a class chart that you have prepared. Make photocopies of the chart below and send home a copy of the form with each child. Take a few minutes each day and exercise with the children, even though they should also be exercising at home, to help them prepare for the fitness test. At the end of the four weeks, recheck the children by having them perform the exercises. Record that information on your class chart. Collect the "Getting Fit at Home" charts and then meet with each child individually to note any improvements that have been made.

Child's Name

Getting Fit at Home

Dear Parents and Guardians,

During the next four weeks we are working on improving our fitness. Please help your child become stronger by exercising. Once a week for four weeks, please check your child's fitness. Also, during this time, please encourage your child to be active to improve flexibility, muscle strength, and endurance. Return the completed chart on _____. Thank you for your assistance.

	Week 1	Week 2	Week 3	Week 4
Running in place (How many minutes?)				
Jumping jacks (How many?)				
Hopping with both feet together (How many?)				
Skipping (How many minutes?)				

Toe-to-Toe Game

Engage the class with the action game Toe-to-Toe while fostering coordination skills. Pair off the children and then have the partners stand in a large open area. The leader names a body part along with a specific direction. Each pair of children touch their named body parts together, such as toes to toes while sitting on the floor, knees to knees while squatting down, elbows to elbows while lying on stomachs, hands to hands while standing tall and reaching for the sky, etc. Extra challenge: Specify the right or left body part to touch as an effective way to have students use motions that cross the midline of their bodies. It is recommended that children wear stickers on their right hands so that they can differentiate right from left.

Name _____

To the Teacher: Instead of tracing the words, you may wish to have the child recognize and circle certain letters.

Trace the words.
Color the person.

My Body

head

hand

arm

leg

foot

Sound Off–Let's March!

Conduct a group march or run as a class with a friendly cadence style rhythm so that you and your students are exercising and singing together. Remind them that some kind of exercise should be done daily. Explain that exercising with friends and singing are both fun things to do; when done together sometimes you even forget that you are exercising! Have students count down and include a song to keep the mood light but focused as they move. Many common cadence rhythms can be found on the Web, but you can also make up your own with a simple "Left, left, left-right, left" introduction. Then, use a call and response echo for the easy, fun rhyming phrases. Use these rhymes to incorporate into your cadence the key themes and terms you are teaching in class. *The children may need extra practice keeping step with the "Left, left, left-right, left" introduction.*

See the following examples:

Left, left, left-right, left.
Left, left, left-right, left.
We exercise—we like to have fun.
Miss Tina's class can get it done.

Left, left, left-right, left.
Left, left, left-right, left.
We know our colors, red, yellow, blue.
We know our colors. How about you?

Left, left, left-right, left.
Left, left, left-right, left.
Good health is important. It can be fun.
We eat fruits and veggies. We love to run.

Name

To the Teacher: Instead of tracing the words, you may wish to have the child recognize and circle certain letters.

Trace and Color

Trace the words with a crayon. Color the shoes.

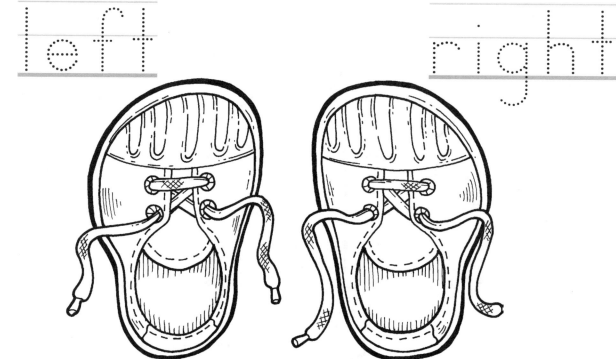

left   right

This Old Man Moves

For this singing and counting game, write the numerals 1–5 individually on index cards. Place each card in a zippered plastic bag. Gather an assortment of 15–20 small objects and place them in a box in front of the class. Choose five children to be the "counters" and hand each child a prepared numeral bag. Teach the class the five verses for the song "This Old Man." While everyone sings the first verse, have the child who holds numeral 1 do a creative dance step up to the box, place one object in the plastic bag, zip the bag to seal it, and then dance back to the group. Repeat the activity in the same manner for verses 2–5. Encourage the singers to perform the specified movements while singing the lyrics. Afterwards, ask other children to recount the collected items in the bags. Repeat the game to allow other children to be counters.

Alternatively, teach your students all 10 verses for this song. The lyrics can be found on the Internet.

This Old Man

This old man, he played one, *(Hold up one finger.)*
He played knick-knack on my thumb;
*(Wave a thumb in the air and
pat it with the other hand.)*
With a knick-knack paddywhack,
give a dog a bone,
*(Cross arms, flap them up and down,
and then extend hand out to offer bone.)*
This old man came rolling home.
(Roll arm over arm while twisting from left to right.)

Additional Verses

Two—on my shoe *(Pick up foot and tap it.)*
Three—on my knee *(Lift knee and tap it.)*
Four—on my door *(Pretend to knock on a door.)*
Five—on my hive *(Pretend to knock carefully
on a beehive.)*

Name

Drawing Spots to Count

Trace the numeral. Draw the matching number of spots on the animal.

Hopping Number Fun

Hopping on a hopscotch grid can be tons of fun. Lay out the hopscotch pattern on the floor using masking tape and then number each square in order from 1–9. Provide each player with a different marker, such as a smooth stone, die, or beanbag. Teach children how to play the game by explaining the procedure and special rules below.

Procedure:

1. Stand near square #1. Toss the marker in that space.

2. Hop over square #1 to square #2.

3. Continue to hop through the hopscotch pattern *on one foot* unless there are two squares side by side; then, jump and land with one foot in each square.

4. When you reach square #9, jump and turn around without leaving the hopscotch path. Then, hop the same way back until you reach square #2. Pick up the marker from square #1 and hop out.

5. For the next round, drop the marker in square #2 and continue as before, jumping over the square with the marker. Repeat until you begin with the marker in square #9.

Special rules: Place your marker back in the square from your previous turn and wait for another turn till the next round if . . . your marker goes in the wrong square, you hop on the square that has your marker, you step on a hopscotch line, you fall over and have to put your other foot or a hand down, or you hop onto a square using both feet.

Name

Hopscotch Numbers

Cut out the numbers.
Glue them in order.

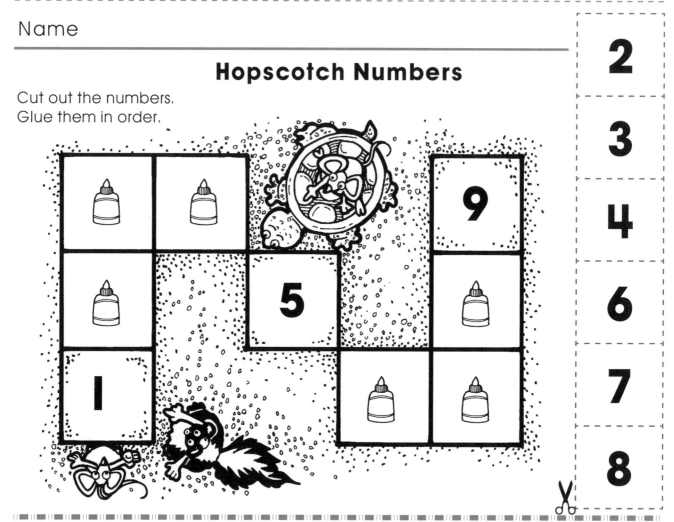

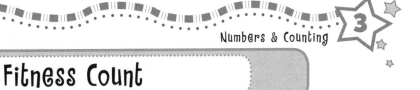

Fitness Count

Have five children stand in a line in front of the class. Choose a type of exercise. The first child does one repetition. Then, the second child does two reps as the class counts, "1, 2," and so on. This emphasizes that "adding one more" means the next number when counting. When five repetitions have been reached, start over again by choosing five different children as leaders. Repeat the same procedure, except this time have the class join in exercising with each leader. Continue until all children have been leaders. Mix up the kids in line and do the activity again. As new numbers are introduced, extend the activity by increasing the number of repetitions to match the numerals.

Examples of Locomotor Movements

arm curls with two small objects	knee bends
crunches	lunges
front leg lifts	push-ups
heel raises	side leg lifts
high knees	sit-ups
hopping on one foot	squats
jumping up and down	toe touches
	toe raises

Name

Dot-to-Dot Counting Fun

Find each animal's path. Draw a line in order from 1 dot to 5 dots.

Captain, May I Count?

Interested in having children work on listening skills and gross motor movements? Let them play the game Captain, May I? Have the children line up side by side. Explain that you will play the captain and stand about 10 feet away facing them. Then, call on a child by name and tell him to come forward or to move back a certain number of steps using a specific movement (giant steps, tiptoes, hops, etc.). For example, say, "Kyle, you may take five baby steps forward." The student must respond with "Captain, may I?" As the captain, you reply either "yes" or "no," and the student must then follow your instructions. Have the other players count the steps aloud. Be sure to emphasize the number of steps each student correctly takes. If the student forgets to ask "Captain, may I?" he must return to the starting line. The game ends after everyone has reached the captain.

Name _____

Stepping with Numbers

Color the steps taken by each player. Circle the player who is closest to the boat.

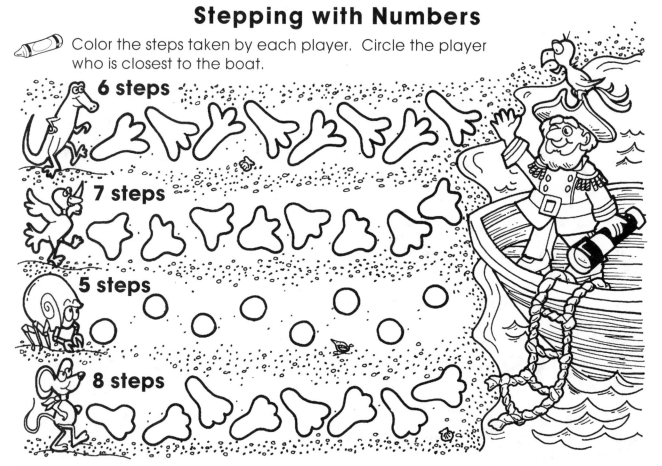

6 steps

7 steps

5 steps

8 steps

Number Jumping

Teach students the tune of the classic song "One Little, Two Little, Three Little Indians," changing the word *Indians* to *jumpers*. Ask 10 children to stand in front of the class. Assign each chosen child a number from 1 to 10; then, have those students squat down to the floor like frogs. You may help students remember their numbers by keeping the line of students in numerical order and pointing to each new jumper in turn. Explain that as the class sings the song aloud, the same number of children will hop up as the number being sung. The first child will jump up on the words "one little." The first and second children will jump on "two little." The first, second, and third children will jump up and down on "three little," and so on up to "ten little jumping kids."

Ten Little Jumpers

One little, two little, three little jumpers,
Four little, five little, six little jumpers,
Seven little, eight little, nine little jumpers,
Ten little jumping kids.

Ten little, nine little, eight little jumpers,
Seven little, six little, five little jumpers,
Four little, three little, two little jumpers,
One little jumping kid.

Name

Lively Numbers in the Pond!

Count the animals.
Draw a line to the number.

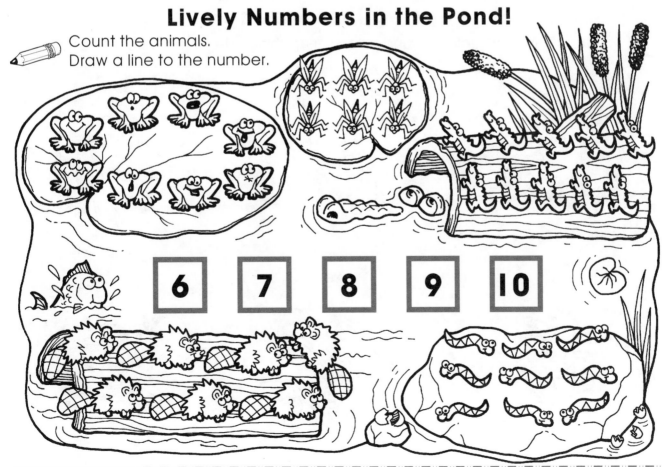

Pocketful of Springtime

Sing a new version of the rhyme "Ring Around the Rosie," adapting new actions as you change the lyrics to incorporate your own spring words. Start with the original rhyme and teach children new verses as they circle holding hands, jump, dance, and learn.

Ring Around the Rosie

Ring around the rosy,
A pocketful of posies,
Ashes, ashes,
We all fall down!

Ring around the rainbow,
A pocket with a daisy,
Springtime, springtime,
Let's dance like crazy!

Ring around the garden,
A pocket with a poppy,
Springtime, springtime,
Let's all get hoppy!

Ring around the blue sky,
A pocket with a raindrop,
Springtime, springtime,
Watch us wiggle nonstop!

Name

Spring Has Sprung

 Draw rainbow circles around each spring thing. Use three different colors.

Serve Up Some Summer

Celebrate the summer season with a modified, indoor version of the classic game volleyball. To make the game much more enjoyable for young children and emphasize the summer theme, decorate the room with beach-inspired decorations, such as plastic shovels and pails and a large sun cutout. Set up a badminton net low to the floor or make your own with several rows of colorful crepe paper. Divide the class into two teams and have each team sit on their bottoms on either side of the net. Explain that they will play a game much like volleyball, tapping a ball back and forth across the net, except they will use a beach ball, and they must stay on their bottoms during play. As children tap the ball back and forth, have them count aloud how many times the ball is touched. Keep the game fun and light. If the ball lands on the floor, simply toss the ball back into the air to begin the counting again.

Name

To the Teacher: Introduce objects that have circular shapes before letting the child complete the page.

Beach Fun

 Use a yellow crayon to trace each path.
Look for circles. Use a red crayon to trace each circle.

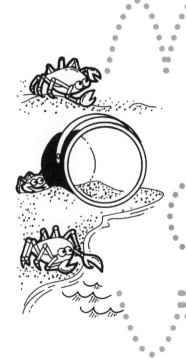

Falling for Fun

Begin this fun fall activity by scattering yellow, red, and brown leaf cutouts all over in a large space. Place three containers, one for each color, around the edges of the space. Divide the class into three groups. Assign the first group to pick up just the yellow leaves, the second group to pick up only red leaves, and the third group to pick up brown leaves. As children gather the leaves, they may hold only one leaf at a time and must skip or hop (or another locomotor movement) when carrying leaves to the correct containers. Alternatively, when all leaves have been collected, ask each group of children to count their leaves and then tell the class that total. Change the task by assigning each team a different color and then play the game again. You might wish to add or remove a few of each color of leaf so that the total is always different.

Name

Fall Go Togethers

 Draw lines to match things that go together.
Color each leaf a different color.

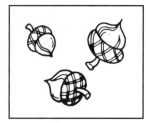

Musical Mittens

Let children match mittens and move to the music as a fun way to foster visual discrimination skills. To prepare for the activity, collect enough pairs of mittens so that each child will be able to wear one of the mittens. Place the mittens in a pile on the floor. Have the class stand in a circle around the mittens. On your signal, everyone picks up a mitten and puts it on. Explain to the children that they must search for the classmate who is wearing the matching mitten. When everyone has found a partner, play winter music like "Jingle Bells," "Frosty the Snowman," "Winter Wonderland," "Let It Snow," and "Sleigh Ride." Let children do a winter dance with their partners while holding mittened hands.

Whenever the music is stopped, the children return their mittens to the pile and then play the game again by choosing a new mitten. Alternatively, have children tell their partners the colors of their mittens before starting the dance music.

Name

Winter Fun

 Draw lines to match the winter pictures.

Nature Walk and Talk

On a sunny day, take students outside for a nature walk. Encourage them to use their senses of sight, smell, hearing, and touch. Have your students focus on each sense for a few minutes. Ask them questions to help them compare the walk to experiences they would have during another season. For example, if it is winter, ask, "What do you see today that you wouldn't see in the summertime?" or "What do you hear right now that you only hear in the winter?" If children do not recognize key sights, smells, sensations, and sounds, point them out, such as, "Do you see the bunny tracks here in the snow? We can tell where the rabbit went in the winter because there is snow." After the nature walk, you may wish to serve a simple, healthful, season-specific snack, such as popcorn in the winter, apple slices in the fall, berries in the spring, or cherry tomatoes in the summer.

Name _____

To the Teacher: You may wish to have the child draw a summer picture on the back of this paper.

Look and Match

Cut out the boxes. Paste them to finish the pictures.

Stick-On Shapes

Learning to identify and match shapes in different sizes is another important concept that can be practiced in a fun way. Find six or more table tennis or other small, plastic, lightweight balls. On each ball draw a different shape (circle, square, triangle, star, oval, rhombus, etc.). Cut out large matching shapes from poster board. Attach a piece of hook-and-loop tape to the blank side of each ball. Place the matching piece of hook-and-loop tape on the corresponding poster board shape. Post the large prepared shapes on a wall or low bulletin board. Allow several children at a time to choose a ball and run (or hop, tiptoe, or other movement) to the poster board shapes to make a match by attaching the ball to the same shape.

To the Teacher: For additional skill practice, let the child color the squares red, the circles blue, and the triangles yellow.

Name

Draw the Shape

 Draw the matching shape in the box.
Draw lines to match the same kind of shapes.

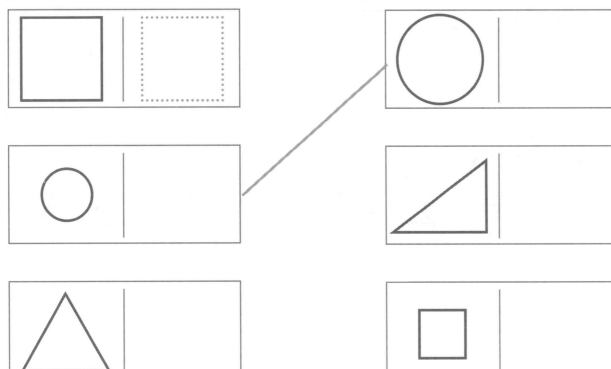

Shape Search

Hide the various pieces from a shape puzzle throughout the room. Explain to the class that everyone must look all over the room for the pieces while walking on tiptoes. When a shape piece is found, have the child bring it to you, name the shape, place it in the puzzle, and do five high fives to celebrate the shape find. Continue until all of the pieces have been found. Repeat the activity with the same or a different shape puzzle. Be sure to change the celebration move for children to use when locating a puzzle piece. Alternatively, if children can count the sides of rectangles, squares, triangles, and rhombi, have them perform the corresponding number of movements (e.g., three jumping jacks for a triangle)

when retrieving a puzzle shape. Alternatively, hide shapes cut from poster board around the room.

Name

Look and Color

Color only the shapes that are the same kind.

Shape Bingo

Play a simplified bingo game. Enlarge the pattern below 125% and then copy the cards on card stock, making one for each child. Divide the class into groups of four children and give each child a bingo card. Provide each player with counters to use as bingo chips. As you call out and/or show a shape, children will place a marker on the matching shape, trying to cover three boxes in a row across, down, or diagonally. When a player wins a game, that player may choose an exercise, such as five toe touches, that the rest of the class must perform. There will be a winner for each group of children. Play enough rounds so that the class has had a mini workout!

Top Shape

For this lively shape activity, cut out three or four examples of each simple geometric shape (square, rectangle, triangle, rhombus, and circle) from poster board. Give each child a prepared shape and then direct the children to find others who are holding the same shapes. Challenge the children in each team to form their designated shape by lying down on the floor and bending, twisting, or straightening their bodies. If possible, take aerial pictures of the groups to show them how well their shapes turned out. Alternatively, you may choose to divide the class in half and have one group see the giant-size shape while the others make it. This is a good time to investigate the difference between squares and rectangles that are not squares.

Name

To the Teacher: Encourage the child to finish the eyes by drawing dots. Teeth can be drawn in the smallest rectangle and eyebrows can be added.

A Funny Face

Use a crayon to trace each shape. Use a different color to make a smaller shape inside of the larger one. Do this step again with another color. Add details to the face.

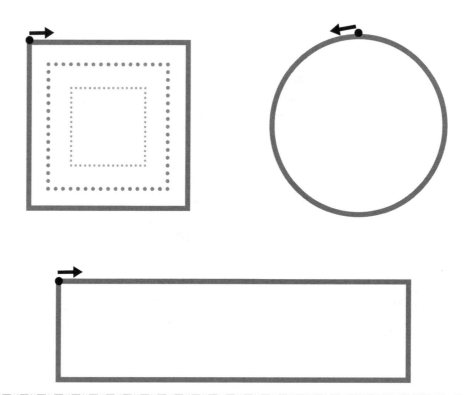

Shape Sort Relay

Sorting shapes into groups can be a lot of fun. For this relay, cut out 10 of each basic shape—square, rectangle, triangle, rhombus, circle, and oval—in different sizes and colors from corrugated cardboard. Put all prepared shapes in a large paper grocery bag. Divide the class into teams of five children and have the teams line up behind the starting line. Set a cardboard box and an empty ice cream bucket a short distance from the relay lines. Explain that the box is for shapes having sides (they are straight and meet at corners) and the bucket is for shapes without sides. Let each child draw a shape from the paper bag. Have the first player in each line high-step march (or another locomotor movement) to the containers and

drop the shape in either the box or bucket. Continue the game until all children have completed the task.

Alternatively, set up a shape toss game using the prepared shape manipulatives. Find a large cardboard box. Cut out the same geometric shapes (they must be larger than the game pieces) from the top of the box. Lean the box against a wall. Designate a spot for the children to stand. Let children take turns trying to toss the game pieces into the matching shape holes.

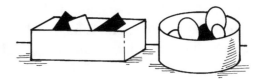

Name _____

Counting Sides

Trace each shape. Count the sides. Write the number.

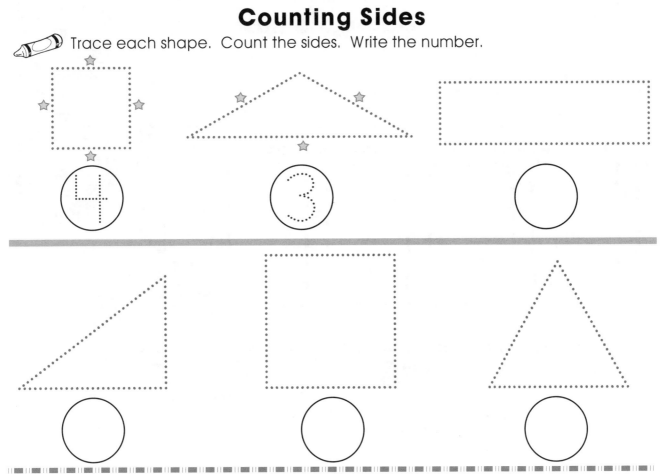

The Bus Gets Moving

Begin the activity by having the class stand in a circle formation. Announce that you are the bus driver, and the students are the bus riders. Introduce the classic song "The Wheels on the Bus" and invite them to follow your lead and have fun riding on the bus. Start to walk around the circle, driving the bus. Then, when you begin to sing the song (see the words below) or play the song on a CD player, stop and have everyone stand facing the center of the circle.

The Wheels on the Bus

The wheels on the bus go round and round,
round and round, round and round.
The wheels on the bus go round and round
all through the town. *(Roll arms and hands around and around in front of the body.)*

Additional Verses

The door on the bus goes open and shut. . . .

The wipers on the bus go swish, swish, swish. . . .

The horn on the bus goes beep, beep, beep. . . .

The people on the bus go up and down. . . .

The baby on the bus says, "Waah, waah, waah." . . .

The parents on the bus say, "Shhh, shhh, shhh!" . . .

The engine on the bus goes
sputter, sputter, sputter. . . .

The brakes on the bus go
squeak, squeak, squeak. . . .

(Make up your own body movements for these verses.)

Name _____

To the Teacher: Choose a child to "drive" the completed bus around the room and pick up others as the "passengers."

Riding the Bus

Draw your friends on the bus. Color the bus. Cut out the pieces. Punch holes and use paper fasteners to attach the wheels. Then, make the wheels go round and round.

Traffic, Traffic, Stop 'n' Go!

When needed, police officers must skillfully guide traffic. Use tape on the floor to mark the roads for the "drivers" on scooter boards to use. Include one or two four-way intersections. Choose children to be traffic cops. Give them "Stop" and "Go" signs to hold (which can be made by printing the words on poster board) or show them how to use hand motions to direct traffic. Depending on the number of scooter boards you have, divide the class into small teams. Explain to children that they are going to take a "driving test" by maneuvering their scooter boards along the "roads" you have made. Then, have the first driver from each team "drive" a scooter. When the driver returns to the team, the second player takes the scooter board to complete the task. Continue the game in the same manner until each child has "driven" a scooter board. Be sure to play the game several times so that all interested children can direct the traffic.

Name

Which Way to Drive?

Trace the path through the maze to the STOP sign.

Go

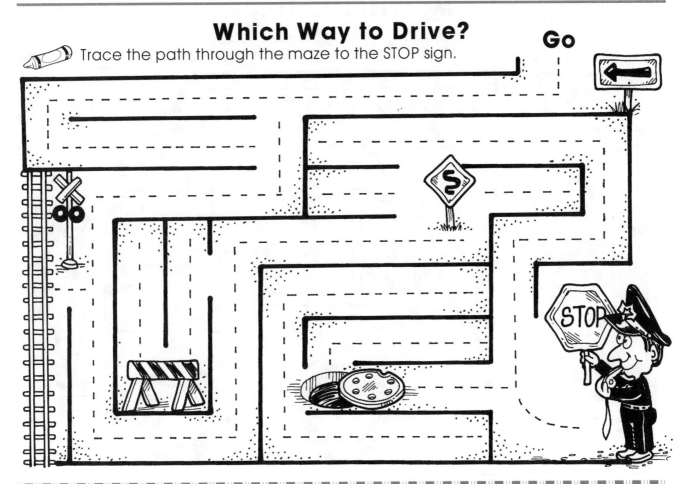

Being Fit to Fight Fires

Have children pretend to be actual firefighters. Using masking tape on the floor, make a simple obstacle course for a fire-fighting team to navigate on scooter boards to reach a large cardboard box "building" that may be painted to look ablaze. Then, tape the shape of a ladder on the floor in front of the building. Set a short length of clean garden hose near the ladder. Explain to the class what hard physical work it is to fight a fire. Have small groups of children take turns working together as a team to find and "put out" the fire. After the alarm is sounded, the firefighters "drive" to the scene on scooter boards and then carry the garden hose "up the ladder" by stepping on each rung. When the fire has been extinguished, the team returns to the station on their scooter boards, so that the next team can answer the call for help.

Name

My Fast Fire Truck

Color and cut out the fire truck parts. Glue the parts together on a sheet of paper.

Pilot Practice

Budding pilots will enjoy this game. Find eight toy planes and eight table tennis or other small, lightweight balls. On each ball draw a different alphabet letter. Cut out large matching letters from poster board. Attach a piece of hook-and-loop tape to the blank side of each ball. Place the matching piece of hook-and-loop tape on the corresponding poster board letter. Post the large prepared letters on a wall or low bulletin board. Allow several children at a time to choose a ball and a plane and slide their feet for a smooth flight to the "airport" (the display of poster board letters). Children then make matches by attaching their balls to the letters. If the match is correct, the pilot "flies" the plane back to the starting line. Repeat the game until all children have carefully flown planes.

Name _____

What's Missing at the Airport?

 Circle **four** things in the first picture that are not in the second picture.

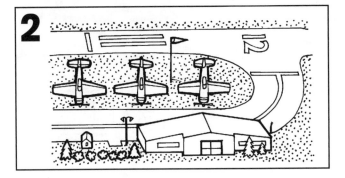
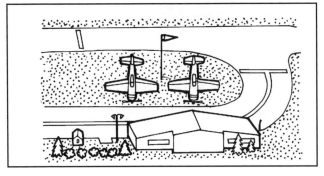

Crafty Conductors

A train conductor has many jobs—coordinating the movements of the train crews, reviewing the schedules and plans related to the train and other trains around it, inspecting the train's cars for safety, handling last-minute changes and problems, helping passengers, collecting tickets, and making announcements. Let children listen and follow directions to practice being a multitasking conductor. Have children line up, one behind the other. Start with one student passing a toy plastic train engine over his head to the next student in line. This continues down the line of children. Then, begin passing a toy plastic train caboose at the other end of the line. Instruct the class to listen carefully to your commands, being prepared

at any time to change the direction of the passing or to complete another movement, such as a hop or side twist, while keeping the engine and caboose moving up and down the relay line.

Name

Look and Circle

 Circle the train engine in each row that is different.

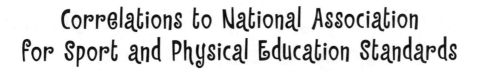

Correlations to National Association for Sport and Physical Education Standards

Fun, Fitness & Learning supports the National Association for Sport and Physical Education *National Standards for Physical Education.*

Certain large group activities support the following Standards and Sample Performance Outcomes for K–2 Students:

A physically educated child . . .

Standard 1: Shows skill in movement skills and patterns needed for a variety of physical activities.

1. **Skips, hops, gallops, slides, tiptoe, etc., using proper form.**

   Many of the activities in *Fun, Fitness & Learning*, which incorporate locomotor skills, support this outcome.

2. **Makes smooth transitions between different kinds of movement in time to music.**

   In this book, several activities that incorporate dancing or moving to music support this outcome.

3. **Balances on different body parts, like a statue.**

   The "Feelings Freeze Tag" activity supports this outcome.

Standard 2: Understands movement concepts, principles, strategies, and tactics as they apply to learning and doing physical activities.

1. **Correctly identifies body parts such as knee, foot, arm, palm, etc.**

   The "Head, Shoulders, Knees, and Toes" activity supports this outcome.

Standard 3: Regularly takes part in physical activity.

1. **Participates in moderate to vigorous physical activity on a regular basis.**

   Most of the large group activities in this book encourage moderate to vigorous physical activity.

2. **Takes part in a variety of physical activities that include the manipulation of objects (such as tossing a ball) both in and outside physical education class.**

   This book includes several games that involve tossing objects such as balls, balloons, or beanbags.

Standard 4: Attains and preserves a healthy level of physical fitness.

1. **Participates in a group of locomotor activities (including hopping, walking, jumping, galloping, and running) without getting tired easily.**

   Many of the large group activities in *Fun, Fitness & Learning* support this outcome.

2. **Takes part in different games that increase breathing and heart rate.**

   Many large-group activities support this outcome.

3. **Knows that physical fitness consists of several different components.**

   The "Moving Our Bodies to Be Fit" chapter supports this outcome.

Standard 5: Shows self-respect and respect for others while participating in physical activity.

1. **Follows directions for all-class activities.**

   All activities in *Fun, Fitness & Learning* support this outcome.

2. **Uses all equipment and activity space safely.**

   Specific large-group activities support this outcome.

3. **Works in a group setting without interfering with others.**

   All activities in this book support this outcome.

4. **Enjoys exploring movement in tasks done alone.**

   Most of the large group activities support this outcome.

Correlations to NAEYC/IRA Position Statement and the NCTE/IRA Standards

Fun, Fitness & Learning supports the following recommendations from *Learning to Read and Write: Developmentally Appropriate Practices for Young Children,* a position statement of the National Association for the Education of Young Children (NAEYC) and the International Reading Association (IRA). This resource also supports the National Council of Teachers of English (NCTE) and International Reading Association *Standards for the English Language Arts.*

NAEYC/IRA Position Statement *Learning to Read and Write: Developmentally Appropriate Practices for Young Children*

Select activities support one or more of the following recommended teaching practices for preschool students:

1. **Adults create positive relationships with children by talking with them, modeling reading and writing, and building children's interest in reading and writing.**

   The activities in the "Learning the Alphabet" chapter help teachers build student interest in reading through movement.

2. **Teachers promote the development of phonemic awareness through appropriate songs, finger plays, games, poems, and stories.**

   The "Letter Sounds," "Alphabet Animals," and "Side-by-Side Rhymes" activities support this standard.

3. **Teachers provide opportunities for children to participate in literacy play, incorporating both reading and writing.**

   The fun and active literacy games in *Fun, Fitness & Learning* engage students in reading through play.

4. **Teachers provide experiences and materials that help children expand their vocabularies.**

   The activities in this book help build students' vocabularies in many areas, including the area of physical activity and movement.

Certain activities support one or more of the following recommended teaching practices for kindergarten students:

1. **Teachers provide opportunities for children to work in small groups.**

   Several activities in *Fun, Fitness & Learning* are done in small groups.

2. **Teachers provide challenging instruction that expands children's knowledge of their world and expands vocabulary.**

   The activities in this book help build students' vocabularies in many areas, including the area of physical activity and movement.

3. **Teachers adapt teaching strategies based on the individual needs of a child.**

   Because many children learn kinesthetically, the activities in this book are a great way to adapt teaching to individual student needs.

NCTE/IRA *Standards for the English Language Arts*

This book and certain activities support one or more of the following standards:

1. **Students read many different types of print and nonprint texts for a variety of purposes.**

   Students must read words, letters, or pictures for many of the activities in *Fun, Fitness & Learning.*

2. **Students use a variety of strategies to build meaning while reading.**

   In this book, several activities focus on many reading skills, including vocabulary, classification, letter and picture identification, phonemic awareness, and rhyming.

3. **Students communicate in spoken, written, and visual form for a variety of purposes and a variety of audiences.**

   While doing the activities in *Fun, Fitness & Learning,* students communicate both verbally and visually (through movement during games and by drawing and cutting and pasting on worksheets.)

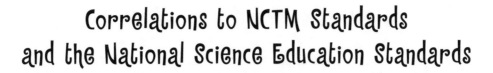

Correlations to NCTM Standards
and the National Science Education Standards

Fun, Fitness & Learning supports the National Council of Teachers of Mathematics (NCTM) *Principles and Standards for School Mathematics* and the *National Science Education Standards*.

NCTM *Principles and Standards for School Mathematics*

Select activities support the following Number and Operations Standard Expectations for Grades Pre-K–2:

1. **Students count and recognize the number of objects in a set.**

   The activities in the "Numbers and Counting" chapter, among others, support this standard.

2. **Students understand the relative position and size of ordinal and cardinal numbers.**

   The activities in the "Numbers and Counting" chapter support this standard.

Select activities support the following Algebra Standard Expectations for Grades Pre-K–2:

1. **Students sort, classify, and order objects by a variety of properties.**

   The "Matching Go-Together Cards," "Side-by-Side Rhymes," and "Shape Sort Relay" activities support this standard.

2. **Students recognize, describe, and extend simple sound, shape, or numeric patterns and change patterns from one form to another.**

   The "Moving for Patterns" activity supports this standard.

Select activities support the following Geometry Standard Expectations for Grades Pre-K–2:

1. **Students identify, create, draw, compare, and sort two- and three-dimensional shapes.**

   Activities in the "Identifying Simple Shapes" chapter support this standard.

2. **Students can interpret the relative position of objects.**

   The "Over-Under-Over-Under" activity supports this standard.

3. **Students describe, name, and interpret direction and distance and use ideas about direction and distance.**

   For many of the activities that involve locomotor movements or tossing, students must use ideas about direction and distance.

National Science Education Standards

Select activities support the following Science as Inquiry Standard for Grades K–4:

1. **All students should develop the ability to do scientific inquiry.**

   The activities in the "Using the Five Senses" chapter support this standard.

Certain activities support the following Physical Science Content Standard for Grades K–4:

1. **All students should understand concepts related to the position and motion of objects.**

   Activities throughout *Fun, Fitness & Learning* support this standard.

Select activities support the following Life Science Content Standards for Grades K–4:

1. **All students should understand the characteristics of organisms.**

   Activities in the "All About Me," "Recognizing Emotions," "Using the Five Senses," and "Moving Our Bodies to Be Fit" chapters support this standard.

2. **All students should understand the relationship of organisms and environments.**

   Activities in the "Thinking About the Seasons" chapter support this standard.

This book and certain activities support the following Science in Personal and Social Perspectives Standard for Grades K–4:

1. **All students should develop understanding of personal health.**

   The large group activities support the standard by encouraging movement and physical fitness.

Correlations to Head Start Framework

The following indicators are used with permission: U.S. Department of Health and Human Services, Administration on Children, Youth and Families/Head Start Bureau. *The Head Start Path to Positive Child Outcomes*. Washington, D.C.

The activities in this book support the following indicators in *The Head Start Child Outcome Framework*:

Language Development: Listening & Understanding

- Demonstrates increasing ability to attend to and understand conversations, stories, songs, and poems.
- Shows progress in understanding and following simple and multiple-step directions.
- Understands an increasingly complex and varied vocabulary.
- For non-English-speaking children, progresses in listening to and understanding English.

Language Development: Speaking & Communicating

- Develops increasing abilities to understand and use language to communicate information, experiences, ideas, feelings, opinions, needs, and questions, and for other varied purposes.
- Progresses in abilities to initiate and respond appropriately in conversation and discussions with peers and adults.
- Uses an increasingly complex and varied spoken vocabulary.
- For non-English-speaking children, progresses in speaking English.

Literacy: Phonological Awareness

- Shows increasing ability to discriminate and identify sounds in spoken language.
- Shows growing awareness of beginning and ending sounds of words.
- Progresses in recognizing matching sounds and rhymes in familiar words, games, songs, stories, and poems.

Literacy: Early Writing

- Experiments with a growing variety of writing tools and materials, such as pencils, crayons, and computers.
- Progresses from using scribbles, shapes, or pictures to represent ideas, to using letter-like symbols, to copying or writing familiar words such as their names.

Literacy: Alphabet Knowledge

- Shows progress in associating the names of letters with their shapes and sounds.
- Identifies at least 10 letters of the alphabet, especially those in their names.

Mathematics: Number & Operations

- Demonstrates increasing interest and awareness of numbers and counting as a means for solving problems and determining quantity.
- Begins to associate number concepts, vocabulary, quantities, and numerals in meaningful ways.
- Develops increasing ability to count in sequence to 10 and beyond.
- Begins to make use of one-to-one correspondence in counting objects and matching groups of objects.
- Develops increased abilities to combine, separate, and name "how many" concrete objects.

Mathematics: Geometry & Spatial Sense

- Begins to recognize, describe, compare, and name common shapes, their parts, and attributes.
- Shows growth in matching, sorting, putting in a series, and regrouping objects according to one or two attributes, such as color, shape, or size.
- Builds an increasing understanding of directionality, order, and positions of objects and words such as *up, down, over, under, top, bottom, inside, outside, in front,* and *behind.*

Mathematics: Patterns & Measurement

- Enhances abilities to recognize, duplicate, and extend simple patterns using a variety of materials.
- Shows increasing abilities to match, sort, put in a series, and regroup objects according to one or two attributes, such as shape or size.

Science: Scientific Skills & Methods

- Begins to use senses and a variety of tools and simple measuring devices to gather information, investigate materials, and observe processes and relationships.
- Develops increased ability to observe and discuss common properties and differences and similarities among objects and materials.
- Develops growing abilities to collect, describe, and record information through a variety of means, including discussion, drawings, and charts.

Science: Scientific Knowledge

- Expands knowledge of and abilities to observe, describe, and discuss the natural world, materials, living things, and natural processes.
- Expands knowledge of and respect for their bodies and the environment.

Creative Arts: Music

- Participates with increasing interest and enjoyment in a variety of music activities, including listening, singing, finger plays, and games.

Social and Emotional Development: Self-Concept

- Begins to develop and express awareness of self in terms of specific abilities, characteristics, and preferences.

Social and Emotional Development: Self-Control

- Demonstrates increasing capacity to follow rules and routines and use materials purposefully, safely, and respectfully.

Social and Emotional Development: Cooperation

- Increases abilities to sustain interactions with peers by helping, sharing, and discussion.
- Develops increasing abilities to give and take in interactions; to take turns in games or using materials; and to interact without being overly submissive or directive.

Social and Emotional Development: Knowledge of Families & Communities

- Develops ability to identify personal characteristics including gender and family composition.
- Develops growing awareness of jobs and what is required to perform them.

Approaches to Learning: Engagement & Persistence

- Grows in abilities to persist in and complete a variety of tasks, activities, projects, and experiences.
- Shows growing capacity to maintain concentration over time on a task, a question, a set of directions, or interactions—despite distractions and interruptions.

Approaches to Learning: Reasoning & Problem Solving

- Develops increasing abilities to classify and compare and contrast objects, events, and experiences.

Physical Health & Development: Fine Motor Skills

- Develops growing strength, dexterity, and control needed to use tools such as scissors, paper punch, stapler, and hammer.
- Grows in hand-eye coordination in building with blocks, putting together puzzles, reproducing shapes and patterns, stringing beads, and using scissors.
- Progresses in abilities to use writing, drawing, and art tools including pencils, markers, chalk, paintbrushes, and various types of technology.

Physical Health & Development: Gross Motor Skills

- Shows increasing levels of proficiency, control, and balance in walking, running, jumping, hopping, skipping, marching, and galloping.
- Demonstrates increasing abilities to coordinate movements in throwing, catching, kicking, bouncing balls, and using the slide and swing.